Prone To Panic

Prone To Panic

Evelyn Gaughan

iUniverse, Inc.
New York Lincoln Shanghai

Prone To Panic

Copyright © 2005 by Evelyn Gaughan

All rights reserved. No part of this book may be used or reproduced by any means, graphic, electronic, or mechanical, including photocopying, recording, taping or by any information storage retrieval system without the written permission of the publisher except in the case of brief quotations embodied in critical articles and reviews.

iUniverse books may be ordered through booksellers or by contacting:

iUniverse
2021 Pine Lake Road, Suite 100
Lincoln, NE 68512
www.iuniverse.com
1-800-Authors (1-800-288-4677)

ISBN-13: 978-0-595-36436-7 (pbk)
ISBN-13: 978-0-595-80868-7 (ebk)
ISBN-10: 0-595-36436-5 (pbk)
ISBN-10: 0-595-80868-9 (ebk)

Printed in the United States of America

Contents

Introduction		ix
CHAPTER 1	My story	1
CHAPTER 2	Why is this happening to me?	5
CHAPTER 3	The science bit	9
CHAPTER 4	First steps	13
CHAPTER 5	Mind over matter	18
	Therapy 101	18
	Physiology 101	21
CHAPTER 6	Self help	25
	Counselling Homework	27
	Support groups	29
	Alternative medicine	30
CHAPTER 7	Setbacks	33
CHAPTER 8	The new you	37
CHAPTER 9	Inspirational writings	40
References		43

Acknowledgements

I am truly thankful to all of the angels who have guided and helped me along the way.

Introduction

There are so many people in the world today who are suffering and alone, unable to talk to anyone about what they are feeling for fear of being rejected. Society has very clear lines about what is acceptable and what is not, but perhaps it is this rigidity and inability to celebrate our uniqueness that causes many of today's illnesses.

I began writing this book about a year after I was diagnosed with Social Anxiety, as I felt there was a total lack of information on this increasingly widespread issue. Over the past two years I have compiled quite an extensive resource book, relevant to what I found useful as someone experiencing panic and anxiety first hand. In my own search for answers, I found a lot of doorstoppers, full of medical jargon and written by 'professionals' who had never actually experienced a panic attack. Cold and clinical in their approach, they left me feeling confused and misunderstood. I wanted to write a book that was open, honest, and full of empathy, offering hope and support to those who feel isolated by fear. My goal is to dispel the myths and stigma that surround anxiety disorders and give people a better understanding of one of the most common illnesses affecting our society today.

Many books claim to possess easy-to-follow, step-by-step instructions on how to stop panicking; gain self-esteem and wave goodbye to anxiety all in six weeks! I find these types of books very misleading, as there is no quick fix for anxiety. Forcing people into a situation where they believe that their anxiety will abate if they just try hard enough is very unhealthy and creates even more anxiety.

Prone To Panic offers an alternative approach based on self-awareness and acceptance. I hope that my experience will serve as an inspiration to anyone experiencing emotional problems in their lives, and a reminder that you are not alone.

1

My story

I knew that something was very wrong when I found myself leaning against the wall for support and gradually sliding down it. I was in the metro station and thought that I was going to faint, so I reasoned that the best thing to do would be to get as near to the ground as possible. Breathing no longer came naturally and I had to really focus in order to get some oxygen into my lungs. My vision started to get blurry and I was, in a word, terrified. A passer by asked me if I was ok, and I surprised myself by responding that everything was perfectly fine! Despite the utter turmoil I was experiencing, I couldn't have other people thinking I was some kind of weirdo! I had left work early that day with what seemed to be stomach cramps. At first I blamed the chinese takeout I had for lunch, and did not make any connection between my stress levels and a baby shower I was being pressurised to attend that evening. I did not feel like going, but I could not think of any way to get out of it and my friend was someone that I found very difficult to say no to. In fact, I found it difficult to say no to anyone. Still, my feelings could not have manifested themselves into this kind of a physical reaction, could they? I really did not want to go to that baby shower!

However, this was about a year after my first ever panic attack, which took place in March 2001, but at the time I had no idea what it was. I was living in Montreal, Canada and working as an administrative assistant with a real estate company. I had recently been promoted and felt intent on proving myself as a match for the big boys in the office. Unfortunately, I was employed in a good old-fashioned male dominated office, where men were men and women made coffee! In retrospect I wonder why I didn't just leave the company when it became clear that I wasn't being taken seriously, but as with my personal life, I was always so intent on proving myself that I lost sight of why I was doing it.

One morning I had a meeting with my boss and some transport officials regarding a new development. I always felt a little self-conscious at these meetings as, being in Quebec, they were usually conducted in French and my accent immediately betrayed me as being the only foreigner in the room. If I was going to stand out, I wanted it to be for something exceptional like the graphics on my PowerPoint presentation, not for having a funny accent! As I sat down at the conference table in the main boardroom, I nodded and took notes as normal. Then all of a sudden I started to feel very hot. I pulled up my sleeves and swept my hair back from my face, but the flushes seemed to get worse. My mouth became dry, so I drank some water and cursed myself for wearing a woollen sweater. I wondered if anybody noticed me shifting about in my chair. Uncomfortable with the heat and realising that I was going to be in this meeting for some time, I started to get anxious. I tried to focus on the meeting, to hear what was being said, but I couldn't concentrate. Then I noticed my heart starting to pound, faster and faster. Before I knew it, my anxiety had escalated into a full-blown panic and I was sure that if I didn't get out of that room then and there I would faint! It was so surreal, I didn't know what was going on but I knew I had to get out. So I quickly blurted out some excuse and fled the scene, making a break for the ladies toilets. Once I got there, I started to splash some cold water on my face and sat on the counter beside the sink. Then, as quickly as the panic had taken hold, it disappeared. My hands stopped trembling and my breathing returned to normal. I couldn't believe it, I was sure something terrible would inevitably happen and then poof, it was gone! Well, I felt so embarrassed that I had left such an important meeting for what seemed to be a false alarm, that I couldn't go back in. I told some of my colleagues what had happened, but it felt like they didn't believe me. Seeing as I hadn't actually fainted or anything, they seemed to think a glass of water would sort it all out! I, on the other hand, was left in a state of shock and confusion. I didn't know what had just happened, how could my symptoms have been so severe in the meeting and virtually non-existent outside of it. All I knew now was that I felt completely exhausted by the whole experience. I left a message for my boss that I was taking the rest of the day off to go to the doctor's and left the building feeling tired and shaken.

The doctor took some blood tests and told me I was probably suffering from stress. Sure I was stressed, I had just given up smoking cigarettes! Deep down I think I knew there was a lot more going on in my life than the everyday stresses, but I didn't want to face it, and was content to put it down to some freak occurrence fuelled by a lack of nicotine and dislike for my boss.

And so I carried on after that strange day as if nothing had happened. Until a year later when all hell broke loose! I had since changed jobs and was now working for a much more reputable company in the pharmaceutical industry. At this point, my life read like a typical 'chic lit' novel. I had a loving boyfriend with whom I shared a cosy apartment in the trendy side of town. I was earning more money, working in my chosen field of Marketing, taking night courses and going to the gym, just like every twenty-something gal should! All was well, apart from the monthly update meetings I had with my department colleagues in the boardroom. For the first couple of meetings, I was a bit nervous, but I figured this was only natural considering I hadn't been working there very long. I wanted to prove myself as a competent employee by making worthy contributions at these meetings and started putting a lot of pressure on myself to perform. Fortunately, they were only once a month, so I tried not to worry about them too much and just hoped that I would get more comfortable with them as time went on. Then I started to notice the same kind of nervous reaction in my evening class when the teacher would ask me a question. My voice would quiver, my hands would tremble and at times I thought my heart would bounce right out of my chest, it was beating so hard. Then, I started to have these sensations whenever I would go into my boss's office. I would feel trapped; like I was losing control of myself.

I couldn't understand where all of this was coming from. I became increasingly afraid of saying or doing the 'wrong thing' in front of my boss, colleagues and fellow students. I was at a loss as to why I was constantly nervous, tired and feeling like I was running on the treadmill of life and getting nowhere. I was doing all of the things which should have been making me happy, so why was I so miserable?

Well, the final straw was about a week after the baby shower fiasco. I met an old friend for coffee and somewhere between complimenting her holiday snaps and ordering a second cappuccino I started to think, imagine if I had one of those attacks here and now! I only had to plant the seed of thought and it began to run rampant like ivy, choking my thoughts. The fear gripped me and as my friend prattled on I started to have this feeling of unreality, like this wasn't really happening or I wasn't really there. I managed to keep the panic at bay, but didn't hang around long enough for it to return. I made my excuses and got on the bus to go home. I was so distraught; I thought these panic attacks only happened in boardrooms! Now, facing the prospect of this fear infecting every aspect of my life, I felt doomed.

The following day was to be my last day at work. I had separate panic attacks on the train going to work, during lunch with my colleagues, sitting at my desk when people would ask me for something and on the train journey home. I was exhausted, emotionally and physically. After what seemed to be the longest journey of my life, I got home and called the local health centre to make an appointment with a social worker. Then I called my mother to tell her that I was probably losing my mind, but that I was going to get help. At the time, it seemed like the darkest moment of my life because I really thought I was 'going crazy', whatever that means. But now I look back on that day as the start of a very long and rewarding journey and think how brave I was to admit that I needed help.

Following my appointment with the social worker, I was seen by the doctor, who confirmed that I was experiencing panic attacks. She prescribed an anti-anxiety medication and arranged for me to see a specialist, who later diagnosed the cause of my panic attacks as Social Anxiety. I was then referred to a psychotherapist, where I started to receive some much needed counselling.

Since then, I have been on a long and bumpy ride! I can't say I have found all of the answers, but I have discovered some useful tools and a new way of looking at life, which I hope to share with you. At the start of this journey, all I ever wanted to know was 'When will I get better?' What I really meant was, when will I go back to being my old self, the old self that got me to this point in the first place! So, I had to re-evaluate my interpretation of being 'better'. It's literally been an entire self-makeover, stripping my life back down to the basics in order to build myself up again. I know that we are all looking for a quick fix, but I have yet to find it (and believe me, I've searched high and low!) What I can tell you is that it does get easier, with a little support, information and a lot of patience and understanding, you'll get there!

Three years later, I am still a work in progress, but the difference now is that I can see how far I have come and focus more on what I *can* do, rather than on what I *can't*. I have achieved so much in the past year that I never thought possible before. I started to take art classes, something I never had the confidence to do in the past because I feared that I wouldn't be any good at it. In fact, even on my worst days when I was practically housebound, I could always make it to my art class because I loved it so much! I've written a book, another achievement that I wouldn't have dared to dream about before. So, while it might be a little early on in the book to refer to anxiety as our friend, try to imagine that there could be something positive to come from this experience. Perhaps it is a wake-up call, not a very pleasant one I grant you, but a wake-up call nonetheless. I hope that the next few chapters will take the cover off this often-misunderstood illness and provide you with a starter map to begin your own journey.

2

Why is this happening to me?

Ah yes, the sixty-four million dollar question! And the first of many to which there is only a very vague answer. The experts argue over whether the irrational behaviour associated with Anxiety Disorders is behavioural (something we have learned from our environment) or biological (hereditary; something we are prone to). However, there are no tests you can take to prove either hypothesis, and so it is generally accepted that anxiety disorders can develop as a result of either or both scenarios. I have to admit, I found little comfort in these explanations. I thought my life had been just fine up to that point, I actually thought I had been quite fortunate in many ways. This anxiousness seemed to just hit me out of the blue, like I had suddenly been infected with a terrible disease and all I wanted to know was how to get rid of it! I could not accept that this was happening to me and that, my friend, is what they call denial! My attitude to mental illness was one of scepticism and fear, not too dissimilar from the rest of society. I did not want to be labelled as a 'crazy person', but I soon discovered that these kind of labels and misconceptions are what keeps us in denial and powerless to face our problems.

We tend to think that illnesses such as anxiety and depression are reserved for a sad bunch of down-and-outs wearing long, threadbare cardigans and greasy hair! Not so, it can happen to anyone, anywhere and at anytime in their life. Just as alcoholism is not restricted to the homeless people on park benches drinking out of a paper bag, mental illness can affect anyone. The problem is that nobody talks about it and so they keep it hidden, afraid of being judged. This is such a shame because, as I found when I started to tell people about my experience, most people are very understanding and have more often than not experienced a similar episode in their own lives. It is nothing to be ashamed of and is far more common than you would expect.

The following is an excerpt from the 2001 World Health Report entitled "Mental Health: New Understanding, New Hope".[1]

Mental illness is not a personal failure. It doesn't happen only to other people. Initial estimates suggest that about 450 million people alive today suffer from mental or neurological disorders or from psychosocial problems such as those related to alcohol and drug abuse. Rare is the family that will be free from an encounter with mental disorders. One person in every four will be affected by a mental disorder at some stage of life.

Today we know that most illnesses, mental and physical, are influenced by a combination of biological, psychological and social factors. Our understanding of the relationship between mental and physical health is rapidly increasing. We know that mental disorders are the outcome of many factors and have a physical basis in the brain. We know they can affect everyone, everywhere. And we know that more often than not, they can be treated effectively.

Society's perception of mental health is changing, thanks to increased awareness and the publication of studies and reports, such as the one above. However, this is a slow process, which, as you can see, has only come about in recent years and it is therefore not surprising that our attitudes to anxiety may be slightly archaic and ignorant. A recent survey[2] carried out on the public's attitude to mental illness in Ireland revealed that two-thirds of the general public regarded sufferers as being weak-willed or feeling sorry for themselves. As research shows, this is completely untrue, but through ignorance and fear, society has formed these unfounded beliefs, perhaps in order to avoid facing their own fears. It is this kind of stigma that distorts our view of anxiety. If someone is suffering from a physical illness that requires them to be in a wheelchair, we are naturally sympathetic to the difficulties they may face and support their efforts to overcome them. However, if someone is suffering from a mental illness, their difficulties may not seem so apparent and we think it is their fault or lack of willpower that prevents them from overcoming the difficulties they are faced with. I have been guilty of this myself in the past, because I did not understand the psychology of these types of illnesses. For some reason, physical health gains precedence over mental health in our society. We are not taught to keep our minds fit and healthy, yet we're constantly bombarded with diets, low-fat alternatives, gym memberships, pedometers, cholesterol tests, etc. Even our cars get a better service than our heads! It is not surprising that my state of mental health needed a complete over-haul after a quarter of a century of rough terrain!

So what is anxiety? Anxiety is the body's natural reaction to a feared situation or a threat in our environment. Basically, anxiety is what makes us move out of

---

1. World Health Organization Director General
2. Psychologist Siobhan Carrick supported by Aware

the way of a speeding car. It forms part of our basic instinct for survival. One form of anxiety is the common "butterflies in your stomach" before taking an exam, giving a speech in public or going on a first date. Anxiety, therefore, is not some rare disease that we have not yet encountered, but rather an exaggerated version of something we already possess. People who suffer from an anxiety disorder respond to everyday trivial occurrences with disproportionate amounts of fear, worry and terror, as though facing a life-threatening situation. Our response to anxiety is based on the "fight or flight" theory. When we as humans are in danger we either try to defend ourselves or escape from the situation. And so, as anxiety sufferers, the easiest option is usually to run to safety and avoid that place or situation that caused our anxiety in the first place. To give an example, I experienced most of my panic attacks in the boardroom at work, and so I attached a sense of danger to having meetings in the boardroom. However, it was not the boardroom that caused my anxiety, but rather the fear of having another panic attack that led me to believe I was in danger every time I entered one. It is easy to confuse the fear of experiencing a panic attack with the fear of a situation.

I remember a friend of mine avoided driving to work because she was so afraid of being caught in a traffic jam. At the time I couldn't understand how a traffic jam could frighten anyone, but now I understand that the fear of feeling trapped in a situation where one could become panicked and unable to escape can be terrifying. These kind of irrational thoughts and fears lead to a lot of avoidance behaviour, which is temporarily gratifying when you call in sick for work, or walk instead of taking the bus, but in the long term creates more problems and feeds the appetite for fear.

The most accurate way that I can describe anxiety is to say that it is like losing your basic sense of trust in yourself and in the world; that gut feeling that tells you everything is going to be all right. In its' place is an overwhelming sense of worry and fear that everything is going to go wrong and you will not be able to handle it.

But what causes anxiety? How do you go from being a spontaneous, confident person to wondering if you can make it to the local supermarket on your own? Well, getting back to my original debate, anxiety can stem from a combination of biological, and social factors. It can be different for everyone; for example, someone could suffer post-traumatic stress following an incident of rape or a natural disaster such as a fire. For me, it was the culmination of several years' worth of suppressed emotions and then some! Things kept 'happening' to me, and I felt powerless to react. My survival technique was to take all of the pain and hide it away somewhere, so that on the surface I was still the over-achiever everyone had come to expect. Certainly in today's modern society of high stress and even higher expectations, it is easy to see how our life experiences could trigger an anxiety disorder. I think Vernon Coleman gave an apt description of modern life in his book *Stress Control*, saying "Staying alive and healthy today is like staying alive and healthy in the middle of a war". We are certainly under more pressure today living in over-crowded cities where it's every man for himself and materialistic wealth and status take precedence over spirituality and inner peace. Consumer based economies demand that we work more to earn more and spend more. The media feeds off of our insecurities and encourages us to live beyond our means. There is no longer any sense of community. The only reason I ever speak to my neighbours is to tell them to turn the noise down! Time is money, and in the race to become the strongest, the fastest or the most powerful, we have completely forgotten to factor in our needs as human beings to live a fulfilling life.

These environmental pressures alone can seriously damage our mental health. However, low self-esteem, adult child issues and the absence of tools to deal with life experiences compound the issue. A big part of my own recovery was acknowledging a family members' alcoholism and dealing with the domino effect this had on my life and my relationships. Years of denial had made it difficult for me to see my life as it really was. I was living an illusion and as the years went by, it became harder and harder to maintain the pretence. I didn't even know who I was anymore. I had an image of myself, based on the life I was portraying to everybody else, and when I found out that this life was a lie, I lost myself. I was only a shadow of a person, not real. And so I was to discover that the root of my anxiety did not lie with one sole cause. It was a combination of factors, from living with an alcoholic and the turmoil that it entails, to a lack of confidence and hunger for approval.

Everyone is different, and part of your journey is to figure out what is behind your anxiety because, contrary to what I first thought, it isn't a deadly disease that hits you out of nowhere. It is a signal, the body's way of trying to communicate something with you. In my own case, I was so far beyond listening to my needs and wants, that it is understandable why my body gave me such a vigorous jolt as a panic attack to gain some attention! Maybe it's saying you need to face certain feelings that have been repressed, confront people with whom you have had toxic relationships, or to find your voice and speak out. Whatever the case may be, the road to recovery is a long and winding one with many lessons to be learned. Just remember that you are not alone on this journey and there is help out there!

3
The science bit

So, how can you tell if you are suffering from an anxiety disorder or if it's just "stress", the blanket term we use nowadays to explain away every ailment from bad skin to our computer crashing! The following is a list of symptoms that can occur during a panic attack:

- Pounding heart
- Air hunger/choking sensation
- Light-headedness or dizziness
- Nausea or stomach problems
- Flushes or chills
- Shortness of breath
- Tingling or numbness
- Shaking or trembling
- Feelings of unreality
- Terror
- A feeling of being out of control or going crazy
- Fear of dying
- Sweating

It is important to note that none of the above symptoms are harmful. But try telling that to an anxiety sufferer! There lies the difference between regular and irregular levels of anxiety. Someone suffering from an anxiety disorder believes that something bad is going to happen and they have a very strong sense of impending doom. Yet, when the worst-case scenario isn't realised, the sense of dread continues in anticipation of the next attack.

This can be a very scary time for people, especially when they don't know what they are up against. This is probably why it is so common for people to jump to the conclusion, "I must be losing my mind", because that is what it feels like. Hopefully, the information laid out in the following chapters will prove to you, and reassure you, that you are not in the least bit crazy. You are not the only one in the world feeling this way and you will get through this.

In order to understand why we are experiencing anxiety, it is helpful to look at the different types of anxiety disorders that exist. Generalised anxiety, Social anxiety (phobia), Post-traumatic stress, Obsessive compulsive, and Panic disorder. The following are brief descriptions of each disorder.

Generalized anxiety disorder

Generalized anxiety disorder (GAD) is as its name suggests, a general form of anxiety with no specific source. Anything from work, family or money to the mere thought of getting through the day can spark an exaggerated response of chronic worry and tension. People with anxiety disorders are usually aware that their reaction is an over-reaction to the situation, but still cannot seem to shake their concerns. Having GAD means always anticipating the worst-case scenario.

Specific phobia

Most people are familiar with phobias such as arachnophobia, fear of flying or heights. It is an intense fear of something that poses little or no threat to our safety. Regardless of how irrational these fears may seem, facing them or just thinking about facing them can bring on severe anxiety or even a panic attack.

Social anxiety

I could talk at length about this, but it wouldn't be fair to the other disorders! Social phobia, as it is also referred to, is a chronic fear of being watched or judged by others and so results in an excessive amount of self-consciousness and avoidance behaviour, so as not to be embarrassed or humiliated in front of others. The symptoms of the anxiety themselves can become cause for embarrassment. People with social anxiety realise that their feelings are irrational, but facing their fears involves extreme dread beforehand, anxiety throughout and an intense self-evaluation on completion, worrying how others may have judged their performance.

Post-traumatic stress disorder

Post-traumatic stress disorder (PTSD) can develop following a traumatic event such as rape, child abuse or serious accidents. People with PTSD have persistent frightening thoughts and memories of their ordeal, leaving them feeling numb and distant.

Obsessive Compulsive Disorder

This is another common catch phrase in today's society used to describe 'neat freaks' or people who are obsessive about punctuality, for example. However, OCD is somewhat more unhealthy than insisting on keeping your desk tidy. It involves uncontrollable rituals and unwelcome thoughts or images. This can involve excessively checking things, counting or washing things, or having persistent thoughts of violence and fear of harming loved ones. There is no pleasure in performing the rituals, which may take up most of the day, only relief from the anxiety experienced when they are not performed.

Panic Disorder

Panic disorder can cause feelings of terror that can strike suddenly without warning. The attacks can occur at any time and so this disorder also causes severe anxiety between episodes, worrying when the next one will strike. The symptoms of a panic attack, which I have described above, can genuinely lead people to believe that they are having a heart attack or dying. These types of attacks generally peak within 10 minutes, but the symptoms can linger.

Side effects

There are also some side-affects that can accompany anxiety disorders, and it is not uncommon to develop secondary symptoms such as alcohol and drug abuse. Other disorders include agoraphobia, which is basically a fear of open spaces or leaving the safety of your home; performance anxiety, which is the fear of constantly being judged and thus rating your performance in each situation; and approval anxiety, which is a fear of being rejected by your peers. Once again, these kinds of behaviour are a part of being human. It is completely natural to want your friends and family to appreciate you, and it is not unusual to want to do a good job. However, it is when your hopes and desires turn into demands and high expectations that the problems begin. I couldn't bear the thought of making a mistake in front of anyone and risk looking like an idiot. So I insisted that I must not make a mistake in any situation. As you can imagine, this sort of

[handwritten: AFRAID OF MAKING MISTAKES!]

a demand is next to impossible and inevitably led to the avoidance of any situation where I did not feel in total control, i.e. practically always!

Have you had similar episodes in your own life? The symptoms are unpleasant, but often it is the anxiety about having anxiety that causes the most upset. I beat myself up so often just for having 'caught' anxiety that I should have at least been recognised as a world lightweight contender! Can you imagine a child coming home, upset and crying because they were frightened by a certain situation, and then imagine scolding them for being so weak and telling them that they should be trying harder. That is basically what we do when we beat ourselves up for having a panic attack. Already tired and upset, we launch into a speech about how things shouldn't be this way and we should be able to cope better. If I could give just one piece of advice it would be this: don't be so hard on yourself. Anxiety is not a terminal illness, but it will take time to work through it, so try to accept that this is the way things are right now. If you can do that and throw out the timetable, you will automatically feel calmer and stop timing your recovery.

Sounds easy, but when you are dealing with an anxiety disorder, this can be the most difficult concept to grasp. As a group, anxiety sufferers are some of the hardest working people in the business of mental health! We will do whatever it takes to get better, just tell us what to do and we'll do it. However, ask us to let go of our need to have everything happen the way we want it to and you've lost us! Letting go of the need to control and just seeing things as they are, are the surest ways to reduce anxiety levels, so drop the demands and the unattainable standards that really aren't getting you anywhere except into more anxiety. It's like the anecdote of the fish caught in the net, the more you struggle; the more entangled you become. If you stop fighting against the anxiety and learn to accept that it's here for a reason and is probably trying to tell you something, then you may just find yourself becoming a little less anxious about your anxiety.

4

First steps

The first and most important step to take is arranging to see your G.P. Self-diagnosis is a precarious business and I would strongly advise you to get a professional opinion. Medical practitioners are much more aware of mental illness nowadays, as it is so common in our modern-day society. If they feel a more specific analysis of your particular situation is necessary, they can refer you to a mental health care specialist or a psychiatrist. Either way, visiting your local medical centre is the best starting point. They will inform you of what services are available to you in your area and what line of action you would like to take, pharmaceutical and/or therapeutic. This can be quite a difficult experience, as most of us have been conditioned to be self-sufficient and very proud, but don't make the same mistake I did, believing that seeking help was giving up or giving in. Quite the opposite, recognising that you have a problem and getting help is being pro-active, responsible and very self-sufficient. Those who carry on ignoring the signs or hoping it will go away are the ones who need a reality check. And the reality is that 1 in 4 people will suffer a mental illness at some point in there lives, so there is nothing to be ashamed of and every reason to believe in your recovery.

There are various treatments available to anxiety patients, but the two universally recognised options are psychotherapy and medication (or a combination of both). The most effective form of psychotherapy for treating anxiety is cognitive behavioural therapy. This form of therapy focuses on changing the thoughts and behaviours that cause anxiety. I attended a psychotherapist for approximately 12 months and found it to be of immense help. Just saying my fears out loud helped me to confront them and to deal with them, rather than ignoring them and seeing them as some kind of enemy. In fact, I learned to accept that my body was actually trying to protect me from a perceived danger and so I began to work with my fears rather than fighting against them. That is to say, instead of trying desperately to avoid having a panic attack, I made an agreement with myself that if I started to feel anxious, I would just allow it to happen. The fear of having a panic attack can often be worse than the experience itself, especially if you have already made allowances for it. And it is often the need to make it go away that creates more anxiety!

I learned new coping skills and with the help of the therapist, started to replace my irrational, negative thoughts with positive ones. Analytic psychotherapy can also be helpful in analysing past events which may have led to anxiety and/or other emotional scar tissue. Another form of therapy is exposure therapy, where the patient is exposed to their feared situation on a continual basis in order to lessen their anxiety. I had a tendency to do this myself anyway, because I felt I was missing out on so much in life due to my anxiety that I would attempt to get myself back into everyday situations, hoping that it would eventually get easier and that in the end I would experience no anxiety at all. I think it is a very effective form of therapy, but it should be carried out on your own terms, i.e. you decide when, where, for how long, and how often—not your mother or your good intentioned friend! Facing your fears can be a daunting task even if you aren't suffering from anxiety, so my advice would be—go easy on yourself if at first you don't succeed. Be prepared for setbacks (which I will discuss at length later on), they are part of the learning process and do not mean that you have reverted back to square one, they just mean that you are not ready today, but you might be ready tomorrow. One thing to note is that, actually doing the thing you feared is rarely (if ever) as scary as you imagined it to be. The amount of worst-case scenarios I conjured up that never came true is astounding!

The pharmacological approach to treating anxiety disorders can be quite confusing as there are so many different types of medication out there. Careful consultation with your doctor will be necessary to determine which course of medication, if any, will be most beneficial to you. Basically, you can go down the long-term route with anti-depressants such as selective serotonin reuptake inhibitors (SSRIs), and monoamine oxidase inhibitors (MAOIs). One well-known brand of SSRI would be Prozac. Alternatively benzodiazepines and beta-blockers offer fast relief but are not to be used long-term. I'm not a pharmacist, so I would again advise you to do your own research. However, for the purposes of giving you a brief introduction to the help that is available, I'll explain a little bit about my own experience with anxiety medication. Initially, I was prescribed Clonazepam, a benzodiazepine that helped to numb the anxiety I was experiencing. A more common benzodiazepine would be Valium, which has become a household name. As a short-term solution they worked quite well, and I was able to take them each time I felt a panic attack coming on and they provided an instant response. However, in the long term they do not eliminate the anxiety, only the symptoms and can become addictive. Anti-depressants have also proven to be quite effective for some anxiety patients as well as those suffering from depression. They are to be taken on a long-term basis and it usually takes about two to three months to see any kind of improvement. However, as with most medications, there are side affects, which can range from dry mouth to sexual dysfunction. I am of the opinion that medication is not the only solution and if we are to believe that anxiety is caused by a combination of factors, it only makes sense that a combination of approaches should be used to treat it.

As I mentioned at the beginning of this book, I stopped taking the Clonazepam as soon as I began the therapy sessions and was encouraged to do so by my doctor. I have to say that his belief in me gave me the confidence to face my problems without the use of drugs. This is not to say that medication should be ruled out completely, and as such he continued to monitor my progress over the next six months.

At this point I decided to return home to my family in Ireland. I was feeling very isolated in Montreal, mainly because I had cut all ties with friends and colleagues. I was so afraid that they would alienate me if they knew what I was really going through, and unfortunately I never gave them the chance to prove me wrong. Before leaving, I was obviously anxious about returning to a potentially volatile family situation and confused about leaving my boyfriend and my adopted home. I was worried that my recovery wasn't happening as fast as I would have liked and feared that maybe I had made the wrong decision in not taking medication. The day before my departure, I went to see another doctor and she prescribed me a course of Moclobemide (MAOI). The first two weeks of taking the medication was quite uncomfortable and was accompanied by headaches, lethargy and lots of nausea. I figured it would be worth it in the long run if I didn't have to experience any more panic attacks. This was not the case however. The side effects did begin to ease after a few weeks, but I still had the nausea and some dizziness for good measure. As for panic attacks, I still had them too. I suppose I was a little bit more sedate, but I didn't want to be sedate. I didn't want to have dry mouth either! So in fact, my experience with this particular type of medication proved to me that it was doing little more than dulling the pain…sometimes. Now, there are times when this is exactly what we require, a bit of 'down time' in order to take a rest. I agree with this idea whole-heartedly (I have since found a herbal remedy that provides exactly the same relief, see chapter 6) but what then? So you have numbed the symptoms, but what about the cause of your problem? Again, I am not a medical expert and I do recognise that prognosis should be on a case-by-case basis, but I have to marvel at the increase in sales of anti-depressants in the last 10 years. I do believe that some people greatly benefit from taking these drugs, but I feel that some in the medical profession are far too quick to fill out a prescription and send you on your way, rather than taking the time to assess whether or not your needs would be better served by counselling or alternative therapies.

Personally, I think this increase in consumption is another form of our dire need as a society to find a quick fix where there is none. All these problems will still be there when the medication stops unless we find some new way of coping with them. It has its value as a temporary solution to alleviate what can be frightening symptoms, but without proper counselling, it is just delaying the inevitable—facing your problems. As a final thought, yes medication is beneficial, but don't expect it to do all of the work.

Once you have taken care of the medical side of things, your next priority will be financial. I was terrified that I would end up on the street if I didn't go back to work, but thankfully there are systems in place to offer income support when you are ill. Firstly, you are entitled to sick leave, the duration of which may vary according to your employer and the length of time you have been working with them. Secondly, there may be some kind of income protection provided by your health insurance company. This could translate into a certain percentage of your salary being covered by your insurance. Your third option is to apply for state benefits such as disability pay. All of these options involve a certain amount of red tape, but it is worth it to have some sense of financial security, allowing you to focus all of your energy on your recovery.

After all of the practicalities have been taken care of, you are left with the burning question asked by all anxiety sufferers is "How long will it take?" The answer is, it will take as long as it takes! For some people it may only take a couple of months, for others, a couple of years. Maybe it's a lifelong recovery in which we learn to accept ourselves for who we really are. Either way, it is an experience unique to you, and often incomprehensible to those around you. I found that to be one of the most frustrating obstacles at the beginning of my recovery—trying to explain to my family, work colleagues and significant others what I was going through. This is not to say that you should be over-concerned with explaining yourself, but finding out you are suffering from an anxiety disorder can be a very vulnerable time and it is comforting to have the support of those around you. All too often, I have heard the remark "Everybody gets nervous, you just have to get on with it", or "Snap out of it". That used to really get my back up! But it is very difficult for someone who has never experienced a panic attack to understand the difference between everyday nerves and an anxiety disorder.

No amount of courage or putting your shoulder to the grindstone is going to make any difference, because ultimately it is not the situation causing your anxiety, it is far more deep rooted than that.

The following excerpt is a sample letter to a friend by anxiety author, Jerilyn Ross.[1] I gave this letter to each member of my family before coming home, to explain all of the things that I couldn't.

Phobic and panic disorders are not associated with "insanity", nor are they the results of laziness, selfishness, or emotional weakness. They come from having repeated panic attacks: involuntary, frightening reactions that are provoked by specific situations.

Imagine the terror you would feel if you were stuck standing in the middle of a six-lane highway with cars coming at you at 100 mph. Your heart would race, your muscles would tremble, and your chest would tighten and pound. You'd be weak at the knees and break out in a cold sweat. During that split-second in which you thought you were going to be hit by a car, you would certainly have an over-whelming desire to escape. Now, imagine how you would feel if that same intensity of fear came upon you for absolutely no reason while you were standing in line to pay your groceries, riding in an elevator, or just walking out of your house. Then imagine if the fear reoccurred each time you even thought about that situation.

Knowing that I am with someone who will not force me into a situation that I feel I cannot handle is a great source of comfort to me. Once that pressure is removed, I am often more able to confront the anxiety-provoking situation step-by-step. Knowing that I can leave a situation at any time also helps alleviate my anxiety and makes confronting my fears easier so please allow me that option. Respect my efforts to face my fears, however small these efforts may seem.

---

1. Triumph Over Fear–Jerilyn Ross

5
Mind over matter

In my experience, every panic attack is made up of physical and psychological factors. Racing thoughts are just as much a part of a panic attack as shortness of breath. Through therapy, we can explore where the root of the anxiety stems from. However, when in the grips of a panic attack, it is useful to be aware of the physiological factors involved.

Therapy 101

Despite any preconceived notions we may have about therapy, I feel it is of vital importance to receive some kind of counselling when dealing with anxiety for several reasons. Firstly, as I have already mentioned, it is a very lonely and confusing time, where no-one understands what you're going through, not even yourself. A trained psychotherapist can help you realise that what you are experiencing is quite normal and nothing to be ashamed of. Seeing a therapist provides you with a safe place to discuss awkward issues in a trusting, non-judgemental environment. The therapist is not there to solve your problems for you, but to nudge you forward on your own path of discovery. I think there is this myth surrounding psychotherapy that involves the client spending hours lying on a *chaise longue* blaming all their problems on their mother! For all you cynics out there, I would recommend a book by Joseph Dunn entitled, *Think Like a Shrink and Keep Yourself Sane*. It is quite a comic view of what really goes on inside a 'shrinks' office.

Cognitive behavioural therapy deals with the here and now by tackling belief systems and creating new coping skills. However, as was the case for me, counselling can also be beneficial to find out what past experiences moulded these thoughts and beliefs, and whether or not they are still serving a purpose in your life today. This is not a blame game, but rather an excavation, where we brush away the dust of recent years in order to see the events, and more importantly our perception of them, that made us who we are today. When I first began attending therapy sessions, I didn't believe there was any connection between this bolt that had hit me out of the blue and anything that may have happened in my past. Over time however, I began to see patterns that had been forming for quite some time and realised that this crescendo of anxiety was inevitable.

Even after I stopped receiving counselling, I continued to work on various aspects of my life that I wished to change. This is a marathon, not a sprint! If you suffered a mild heart attack, surely your recovery would not end after the by-pass. You would adopt a healthier lifestyle and commit to more exercise and a balanced diet. Equally, mental health is a commitment to yourself that you will adopt a more balanced lifestyle, where there is plenty of time to focus on your needs. In my recovery, the following issues required a lot of attention and I hope that reading them will spark some questions within you and perhaps give you some direction.

Self-esteem

This is a bit of a slippery fish, as self-esteem can mean so many different things to different people. I always thought I was brimming with self-esteem, until I realised that it was conditional—the condition being that I do everything right and act perfectly all of the time. Up to that point in my life, I was under the impression that things had gone pretty smoothly, so I never had any reason to doubt my self worth. However, when the bottom seemed to fall out of my world, I realised I had no confidence in myself whatsoever. I assumed the identity of a girl I thought everybody would like, and as a result, never gave anyone a chance to get to know the real me. I know it's a cliché, but I believe that self-esteem grows out of loving yourself because of your faults and not despite them.

Accept yourself unconditionally, meaning that no matter what happens, good or bad, you accept yourself. Avoid basing your entire worth on the approval of others or your accomplishments. Obviously, this will not happen overnight, but fortunately there are a lot of courses available on nurturing self-esteem and numerous books at the local library.

It must be one of the most difficult aspects of the recovery process, as it is all-too-easy to regress to the belief that 'I am only as good as my last sale' (to use a retail analogy). However, as human beings we have good days and bad, but this does not mean we are good or bad people. As with others around us, we can reject the sin but not the sinner. It constitutes major progress just to be aware of this and to begin to learn how to love ourselves for who we are, not how well we perform. I am still learning and will probably continue to learn for the rest of my life!

It takes a lot of courage to just be yourself and to let other people love you for who you are, not who you think they want you to be.

Co-dependency

This was the hardest pill for me to swallow. I had always prided myself on my independence; so finding out that I had spent most of my life involved in co-dependant relationships came as quite a shock to me. The flip side was that I now recognised why I was constantly drawn to people with emotional dysfunction and why I always thought I could 'fix' them. It is worth picking up one of Melody Beattie's books on co-dependency, *Beyond Co-dependency And Getting Better All The Time* and *Co-dependent No More*. She explores the roots of co-dependency, whether it be growing up in a dysfunctional family system or living with an alcoholic. So, how do you know if you are in a co-dependent relationship (or ten!) or not? Well, you may find yourself spending copious amounts of time with someone whose company you do not even enjoy because you feel obliged or you feel that they will not cope without you. You may be unable to set boundaries in your relationships, for example, always being available whenever you're needed to do whatever is asked of you. In other words, you have a hard time saying no! You may find yourself trying to control those around you, and losing your temper when they do not obey. One of my warning signs was my inability to cope with conflict of any description and so my main survival technique was constantly giving in to other people's outlandish tempers and demands—basically a doormat! This is care taking for people who create nothing but craziness in your life and make you feel guilty when you're unavailable.

If any of the above scenarios sound familiar, then the chances are that co-dependency could be an issue for you. I hope you will learn from my mistakes and avoid beating yourself up for being a doormat. I used to feel so useless compared to my perfect friends who were well equipped to stand up for themselves—or so I thought. But the only way to embrace change is to forgive yourself for using whatever coping skills you possessed in order to survive. You did the best you could with what you had at the time and now you are going to learn new coping skills as an adult that work for you. Once you achieve awareness, you're half way there. All that's left to do is to work on changing these self-defeating behaviours—piece of cake! Ok, I'm exaggerating, like the whole recovery process, it takes time and patience to achieve these changes, but once the ball has been set in motion, you may find that it is hard to stand by and do nothing when somebody is taking you for granted. All of a sudden, the importance of your own feelings takes priority and you realise your right to stand up for yourself.

Inner child

Okay, now I have pushed it too far! I had you right up until I said the words 'inner child' didn't I? I was just as sceptical about blaming it all on my childhood, but don't dismiss the idea of having a wounded child inside of you straight away.

When my counsellor first introduced the idea of the wounded inner child, I really thought she was reaching a tad too far. As far as I was concerned, I had an ideal childhood. Nothing terrible ever happened to me, I had both of my parents and I got along just fine at school. But children are crafty and you never really know how something is affecting them, as they tend to store away unpleasant situations that they are unable to process. Family dynamics dictate that we all adopt certain roles to keep the family 'balanced'. These roles may be completely dysfunctional, for example, I acted like the comedian in my family to counteract the depressive mood swings of my sister and my father. It wasn't up to me to 'make things better', but I took on this role to deal with our family problems and everybody seemed to love me for doing it, so of course I kept it up.

This is just one simple example of how children are unable to process grown-up problems, and so use their survival techniques to avert danger and be accepted. Imagine all of the things that could have happened in your childhood that you were unable to understand and have never fully faced up to? Pain doesn't just go away, it is stored away in the attic of our minds until we are able to deal with it, mourn for it, accept it and then move on. The best book that I have come across which deals with this topic is *Homecoming* by John Bradshaw. It is full of exercises to help you get in touch with your inner child and work through any childhood hurts that may be lurking in your closet.

Physiology 101

While I believe it is important to ascertain where the root of your anxiety is stemming from, I know that a more pressing matter awaits—how to stop panic attacks! I have leafed through the pages of so many books trying to find the chapter on "what the hell do I do to stop panicking!?", but I never seemed to find it. That's because there is no quick fix and like I said before, the sooner you accept that this is a process, the easier it will be. There are steps you can take, however trivial they may seem at first, which can in fact help you to relax and allay your fears. Deep breathing is your first line of defence. It doesn't sound like much, but it was one of the first things my mother introduced to me from her yoga class and a technique I still use today. It basically involves lying on your back, inhaling to a count of four while your abdomen rises, then exhaling for a count of six. A lot of panic sufferers breath from their chest, which can only hold a certain amount of air and so causes short, shallow breathing. Breathing into your abdomen is slow and allows large volumes of oxygen to be inhaled as you push out your stomach. After some practice, you'll find this technique can be used anywhere at anytime. Like I said, it may sound too easy to be of any use in your battle against panic, but it is one of the most effective tools available.

A panic attack sets off a series of events in the body that is often difficult, if not impossible to stop. Everything is speeded up and your instinct is to run to safety. Ironically, this only encourages the process and sustains the panic. I have found that a good antidote to this is to just sit down and slow down. Instead of running away in fear, sit down on the nearest available seat, have a sip of water and just breathe. This simple action allows the racing thoughts to calm and your breathing to return to normal. You can still leave the situation you are in, but you will be walking away calmer and feeling better. It is interesting to note that on most of the occasions where I have decided to sit down and slow down instead of fleeing the scene, I have actually decided to stay and ended up enjoying my outing.

Exercise is another way to ease anxiety. It is well known that pumping iron releases endorphins and thus automatically lifts your mood. For me, exercise was a great way to take my mind of things and gave my thoughts a well-earned rest. A brisk twenty minute walk allowed my mind to focus on other things like nature, shop windows, buildings and I would naturally feel better for having got out of the house for a breath of fresh air. It's a win-win situation!

But the most valuable tool in lowering anxiety is accepting that the symptoms caused by your anxiety disorder are completely harmless. Once you believe this and dispel the sense of danger you are attaching to these symptoms, anxiety will no longer control your life. I suppose this is the Achilles heel of anxiety sufferers, how are we supposed to believe that the symptoms of a panic attack are harmless when they feel so terrifying and beyond our control? It's not easy, but here's something that may help.

The Anxiety Panic Internet Resource[1] has a page on their website describing the physiology of a panic attack. This was a crucial moment in my recovery because up to that point, I wasn't really 100% sure that these symptoms were harmless. Despite countless consultations with a medical specialist, I still had my doubts as to whether or not these symptoms could actually cause me to faint or hyperventilate. Seeing the symptoms mapped out as a systematic response to a

---

1. The Anxiety Panic Internet Resource–www.algy.com/anxiety

perceived threat in the environment, made me realise that it was the most natural response in the world. I could even see how the symptoms were there to protect me! So, no matter how uncomfortable they may feel, they could never harm me, as they are actually there to protect me from a danger coming from outside the body.

It bases the physiology of a panic attack on the 'fight or flight' theory and demonstrates its importance in the human body by using our ancestors, the cave men, as an example. Basically, the number one purpose of anxiety is the protection of the organism, which was vital for our survival back in the day. So, when there is an immediate threat in our environment, a chain of events is set in motion by the release of chemicals in the brain, adrenaline and nor-adrenaline. These chemicals produce various reactions in the body, preparing it for conflict or a speedy getaway. The heart rate increases, which in turn increases the bloodflow around the body. Blood is pumped to vital organs such as the lungs and the muscles, preparing for action. This means the blood supply is directed away from the extremities of the body such as the fingers and the toes, which explains the tingling sensations we feel during a panic attack and the hot and cold flushes. As the body needs more oxygen to prepare for it's fight or flight, an increase in the speed of breathing occurs. This explains the air hunger, the choking sensations and the light-headedness. A reduction in the flow of blood to the head can also result in dizziness, blurred vision and feelings of unreality. All of these reactions are, of course, completely harmless and actually protecting us. All of these preparations produce a lot of sweating, which is the body's way of preventing ourselves from over-heating. It is also suggesting that sweating makes the skin slippery and so more difficult for a predator to catch!

Other symptoms include a decrease in digestive activity, as all attention is being focused on the 'action' glands. This could be what produces the feelings of nausea synonymous with anxiety. Also, a decrease in salivation produces the dry mouth most people experience during panic attacks. As I am sure you are acutely aware, all of this activity takes it's toll on the body and leaves you feeling drained and exhausted. These symptoms can last anywhere from 5 to 15 minutes, but the important thing to note is that they, without fail, eventually fizzle out. The chemicals produced are eventually killed off by other chemicals in the body which automatically kick in to prevent, for want of a better term, overloading. So anxiety is just a natural process in the body, which is brought about by a perceived danger and is completely harmless—really! It may feel very uncomfortable, but a panic attack will dissipate, as it cannot maintain its momentum for long.

Try to remember that the next time you fear the onset of a panic attack, it is only natural and it will fade away.

6
Self help

I have already discussed the different schools of thought that link anxiety to either biological or environmental factors. There are arguments for and against, but how can we ever really know definitively? My family tree reveals a history of emotional problems and so it could be heredity, but what about all of the difficult experiences in my life that may have caused me to construct unhealthy coping behaviours? I could battle this one out until the proverbial cows come home, but will the answer have any great affect my current situation? Probably not. There is only one part of this equation that I can actually do something about, and that is ME!

One of the happiest days of my life was when I told my counsellor that I was fed up looking to other people for all of the answers and that I had finally decided that my own answers were as good as anybody else's. She discharged me immediately! Of course these magical moments of insight do not tend to last very long and I soon found myself swamped once again in the trivialities of life. Still, I will never forget that first glimpse of what self-help truly means. We may not have any choice as to whether or not we are prone to anxiety, but we do have a choice when it comes to our reaction. We may not be able to control what happens to us, but we have some measure of control over how we react. For example, if I experience a panic attack at the supermarket I can spend the day getting angry with myself; feel cheated out of a 'normal' life and worry about whether I will ever be able to do my groceries again. On the other hand I could sit down and take some time to relax and lick my wounds, praise myself for making the effort and get on with my day. It may not seem so now, but you do have a choice—you are not powerless.

In Albert Ellis' book, *How to Control Anxiety Before it Controls You*, he talks about how things and people alone do not make you anxious—*you* do. I can almost sense your defensiveness! However, it is true that, through our demands and unrealistic expectations of ourselves, we create a lot of our own anxiety. Fortunately, if this is the case, then surely it stands to reason that we also play a pivotal role in diminishing our anxiety. Much of our anxiety stems from the beliefs, or rather irrational beliefs, that we hold about certain things. To use an earlier example, I used to dread making a mistake in front of anybody, and so I insisted that I must always appear professional and competent in any given situation. My belief was that people would think I was an idiot if I messed up. This left me feeling very apprehensive about meeting new people.

Using Ellis' Rational Emotive Behavioural Therapy[1] to challenge my irrational beliefs, I realised that it was unrealistic to expect that I would never make a mistake. Furthermore, I reasoned that people probably wouldn't think that badly of me if I slipped up, and they might even like me more for being a fallible human being rather than being like a robot who always gets it right. I therefore replaced my demands for perfection with a more realistic preference to come across well. Using this approach, I formed a new set of rational beliefs. "I hope that I perform well and that people like me, but if I don't it does not mean that I am a total failure". This new philosophy makes me a lot less apprehensive about meeting people and less likely to rate my performance.

This form of therapy is quite similar to Cognitive Behavioural Therapy, and it is a very powerful tool. It removes the feeling of helplessness and gives us a choice. This, in my opinion, is the key to self-help and has been widely researched as far back as the ancient philosophers. Another title dealing with this topic is *The Self You Have To Live With* by Winfred Rhoades and embraces the idea that, while most things are beyond our control, the world of one's own creating is what makes our experience of the world a pleasant one or a not-so-pleasant one.

However, be patient, as this type of therapy takes a lot of practice. Tackling the belief systems we have spent years creating is no small task. Your thinking will not change just because you want it to. I think the most useless statement ever concocted was 'think positive'! There is no point in lying to yourself, and that is why I find this kind of rational therapy so effective. Ask yourself if things are really as bad as they can be, if you really can't stand it, or if you really cannot accept yourself for being less than perfect. Take the worst-case scenario and ask yourself if it is really that awful. In my own example, the worst-case scenario did happen, and I made an idiot of myself in front of someone that I wanted to impress. I was completely embarrassed, but the other person found it quite funny

---

1. REBT is a form of psychotherapy, which was developed by Dr. Albert Ellis Ph.D. in 1955.

and really warmed to me. My biggest fear of looking like an idiot actually broke the ice with someone I wanted to get to know better and my world didn't end.

This experience taught me something else; if that person had rejected me because of the silly mistake I had made, then they would not be the type of person I would like to associate with. I realised that I would have very little respect for someone who could judge other people on such a superficial basis. It took a long time for me to arrive at this conclusion, and at the risk of sounding like a broken record, take your time. This is a life-long process of learning and one of the most valuable lessons you will learn is that the behaviour is the last thing to change. Even though your thinking may have reached dizzying new heights, it will take a while for your behaviour to catch up. This can be very frustrating, because your mind is telling you not to be afraid and not to worry, but your body does just the opposite. I'm sure you saw this cliché coming, yes folks, old habits die hard! So now that we have questioned everything we ever believed in, what else can we do in order to help ourselves?

Counselling Homework

As I mentioned in the previous chapter, I found therapy to be the cornerstone of my recovery. However, this takes up a mere sixty minutes of your week, so what can you do in the meantime? My therapist encouraged me to keep a journal, in order to act as my own therapist. At first, I was hesitant in trying this technique because I thought, isn't that what I'm paying her for? But it soon became clear that if I really wanted to change my behaviour, I would have to take the control back into my own hands, rather than depending on my therapist or anyone else. I had never even kept a diary as a child and found the whole thing pretty uncomfortable. However, one day I came up against a certain situation, which left me indecisive and unable to take action. So, I sat down and wrote all my concerns and questions on a page and, without even being conscious of what I was doing, started to write a response on the following page. It was like a whole other person was talking to me, but I later realised that it was the rational side of my brain responding to the irrational side. People do this every minute of every day when making choices big or small, they just don't realise it. Because of my anxiety, I found it difficult to think anything through, let alone give my out-numbered rational thoughts any airtime. Writing these racing thoughts down on a page gave them some kind of closure that wasn't possible when they were swimming round in endless circles in my head. Once the irrational thoughts were written down, I could then question them, challenge their validity, pin them down and deal with them. It was one of the most useful tools I came up with. Initially, I suspected I had really gone over the edge—I mean having two completely independent voices in my head? But after a humorous consultation with my therapist, I realised that we all have several voices and several personalities debating every move we make in life. It is just that our rational voice becomes almost inaudible when drowned out by the very powerful negative thoughts and fears caused by anxiety. I would strongly recommend writing your thoughts down, even if it feels strange. Keeping a journal helps you to face your fears and more importantly, come up with your own solutions to them. It's the best way to become more self aware and thereby better able to help yourself.

It took me a while to realise that it was not my counsellor who was doing the work, but me! This is why doing your homework is so important, because nobody knows what has gone on in your life better than you, and nobody else knows what it feels like to be you. Homework doesn't have to be in the form of a journal, it can just be sitting still and thinking about your life. I suppose it is a process of facing up to the reality of your life, rather than the rose coloured still frames you choose to remember. This process helped me to see that there had been several blows to my confidence, which I had never fully recovered from and, if I'm honest, had never even acknowledged. Knocks to our self-esteem, whether they are in our professional life or personal, do not go away when ignored. They stay frozen somewhere in the back of our minds, waiting to be felt and expressed. I had to face up to some really sad truths and incidents that didn't appear to mean that much to me at the time. It turns out that they did mean a lot! But I found they were far less scary once they were out in the open, rather than hidden in the shadows.

The most positive aspect about doing your homework is that you get to know yourself better and become more aware of the kind of person you want to be. Along with the realisations that surface through this new self-awareness comes the over-whelming desire for change and a putting to rights. Changing your priorities and thus your behaviour can mean very confusing times for your family and significant others. People do not like change and can be quite vocal about it! In my case, I knew I wanted to change, and even though I couldn't expect those around me to change, they had to accept that I wouldn't be the same old daughter, sister or girlfriend that I used to be. This period of adjustment was probably more difficult for my significant others than for me, because once I had learned to stand up for my rights, and myself it no longer mattered to me what their reaction was. Yes, I was accused of being selfish, because everyone had become accustomed to me always being there, ready to help and prepared to do whatever made the majority happy. Little did they realise that I was sacrificing my own wants and needs and giving their feelings priority over my own. Expressing your wants and needs is not selfish, so stick to your guns. Remember that your feelings are just as important as anyone else's and you have as much right to be happy as the next person.

Support groups

Fortunately, there are many support groups all over the world for people suffering from anxiety. I was lucky enough to find a **Recovery Inc.**[2] support group where I was living. They operate worldwide and the meetings follow the same structure in every country. My preconceived notions of a support group were something along the lines of the film "One flew over the cuckoo's nest" and the thought of attending one of these meetings was a bit bizarre! How wrong I was. As suggested by the name, these groups offer the kind of support that is unavailable anywhere else. Family, friends, even doctors, may try to offer understanding and support, but unless they have experienced anxiety first-hand, they cannot fully understand what you're going through. In my own case, it was especially helpful to walk into a room full of people (which normally would have been out of the question for me) and sit and talk about my problems without fearing judgement or funny looks. It was a place of understanding and solidarity, encouragement and acceptance.

Not only did this support group provide a safe place to vent, but it also offered learning tools. Recovery Inc. was founded by Abraham A. Low, M.D., who developed the self-help method after many years of research, study and treatment of patients. He wrote several self-help books, including "Mental Health Through Will Training" and "Manage Your Fears, Manage Your Anger", from which excerpts are read aloud at the start of each meeting. I suppose the first positive sign I had that these meetings could work, was the fact that several of the participants had been in attendance for up to ten years! A lot of people found that the Recovery meetings had worked for them and wanted to give back to newer members, as well as continuing to practice Recovery methods in their own lives. Also, the fact that the group leader herself had started out by seeking help at a Recovery meeting for her depression fourteen years previous, gave me an immeasurable

---

2. Recovery Inc. Self-Help Mental Health Since 1937

amount of hope and optimism. In fact, Recovery Inc. is a non-profit community service organisation, which is completely member-managed.

The Recovery method teaches members how to identify and manage the negative thoughts, reactions, beliefs and behaviours that lead to emotional pain and disturbing physical complaints, which have no physical cause. The meetings themselves are very structured and contrary to what I believed; you don't sit there for two hours listening to someone droning on about their problems. Members are invited to volunteer examples where they may have experienced an anxiety-provoking situation and describe how they are using the self-help method to cope better. Then the other members offer further insight into how the Recovery principles were used by the person volunteering the example, and generally offer positive feedback for the efforts made. This is invaluable to anyone suffering from anxiety and/or depression, as it is not always easy to see the positive side of anything. Then the meeting becomes more informal and members talk in smaller groups where they encourage and support each other. It's normal to have reservations about the unknown, but even more so if your image of something has been tainted by society or disturbing old movies! But let me tell you, these are real people with real problems and unlike the majority, are facing their fears and doing something about it. Support groups may not be right for everyone, but you have nothing to lose by giving it a go. Like everything else I have mentioned, it is not a quick fix, and it will take a couple of weeks before you will notice any improvement, but to merely have the opportunity of meeting people in similar situations can be of immense value.

Alternative medicine

There are various other methods I used during my recovery and still do. The most obvious technique for an anxiety sufferer to learn is that of relaxation. Nowadays, there are a million and one ways to learn how to relax (how ironic!). Yoga is a great starting point, as a lot of the exercises are based on deep breathing. One of the symptoms of a panic attack is shallow breathing, and Yoga teaches you to breathe slowly and deeply. As I explained in Chapter 5, this is something that is easy, practical and you can start right away without paying any money or taking any courses. I practiced Sivananda Yoga and found the combination of meditation and deep breathing to be very relaxing. Once you become comfortable enough with this breathing exercise, you can use it anytime you feel anxious. I still focus on my breathing automatically if I feel nervous, be it on the bus or queuing at the bank.

Another great form of relaxation is massage. My cousin introduced me to a Shiatsu massage drop-in centre and I've been going ever since. This massage is performed over clothing, so it might be more appealing to a wider clientele. It is based on the principles of Acupuncture and works on the various pressure points around the body. I found it incredibly relaxing and nurturing. A big part of self-help is learning how to take care of ourselves, and seeing it as a necessity rather than a luxury.

A visit to your local herbalist may also be an option, especially if pharmaceuticals aren't your thing. However, people often make the mistake that herbs are natural and therefore harmless. Self-medicating can probably do more damage than good, so it is advisable to consult a herbalist before taking anything. Herbal remedies are also available over the counter at the pharmacy, such as Quiet Life, which is manufactured by Lanes. I followed a course of this remedy for two weeks and found it to be a very effective short-term relief from the symptoms of anxiety. The major ingredients include Motherwort, Valerian and Passiflora, which are known to promote relaxation. A trip to your local health shop will provide you with many alternatives to ease your symptoms and increase your sense of well-being.

We have all heard the saying "a healthy body is a healthy mind". I have already discussed the benefits of exercise, but I feel enough cannot be said about its positive effects on anxiety. I bought myself a bike, mainly because I used to love cycling as a child. It gave me such a sense of freedom and meant that I could get around even if I didn't feel up to using public transport. When I was cycling, I felt like nothing could touch me, I felt strong and confident. Try to find a sport or an activity that appeals to you, because if it isn't fun the chances are you won't do it.

Also, it is very important to do things that make you happy during this time of anxiety. I know that everyday trivial events can be so draining and filled with danger, that it is nice to do something that pleases you and helps you at the same time. As I keep saying throughout this book, be gentle with yourself. Pushing yourself and forcing yourself into things if you're not ready will only cause more anxiety. You will get there eventually, I promise you!

As well as exercise, you can also look after your body by watching what you put into it. I stopped drinking caffeine as I felt I was wired enough already! People suffering from panic disorders should avoid cola, tea and coffee or drink decaffeinated versions. Plenty of sleep and rest are obviously desirable as well as a balanced diet. Unfortunately, alcohol and drugs can become a crutch for many people suffering from anxiety. Even though they may alleviate some of the pressure in the short term, they usually end up adding to your problems in the long term. Alcohol itself is a depressant and just as addictive as any other class A drug, with equally devastating consequences. Self help also means being responsible for yourself, your decisions and your actions.

7

Setbacks

I am devoting an entire chapter to this subject, because I think it is an area that is often overlooked. Setbacks are those days where you feel as though you are right back at square one, that all of your work has been in vain and that there is no sign of any hope for the future. It can be very disheartening, but rest assured that this is part of the process.

I recently experienced a setback, which started with a trip to the post office. There was a very long queue and I started to become agitated. When I had to queue again at the bank I experienced a panic attack, something I had not had for a very long time. I began to get frustrated with myself, and wondered why this was such a problem today and not yesterday. I thought great; here we go again! Fortunately, I have had so many setbacks that I no longer fear the outcome and I know I will get through it. More importantly, I know it has nothing to do with the bank or the queue or anything else in my environment. The changes are occurring inside and that is where I need to put my focus. If going to the post office yesterday was not a problem and it is today, well it is not the post office that has changed. So I had to sit down quietly and ask myself what was the matter. This can be a difficult process and it takes practice to separate the feelings of anxiety from the root cause. I realised I had run into the same old rut, which consisted of me putting everyone else first and leaving very little time for myself. I was feeling under constant pressure, doing what I thought was expected of me rather than what I wanted. Add a good measure of negativity and racing thoughts about all of the things I cannot do, and you have got yourself a recipe for a hearty bowl of setback! This may seem a bit too simplistic of an explanation for something so complex as an anxiety disorder, but it is the neglect of our basic needs that leads to such consequences. We are the most advanced species on the planet with the most highly developed forms of communication, and yet it is next to impossible for us just to say what we feel, even to ourselves. However, if you can manage to quieten the mental chatter for long enough, you will hear what some people refer to as your heart speaking to you.

Now I'm really going to drop a bombshell on you! The truth is that we would rather get caught up in the whirlwind of panic and anxiety, than face the real source of our pain. As humans, we are programmed to avoid pain at all costs, and experiencing anxiety disorders is the price we pay. It creates a smoke screen, so that we will be too preoccupied to ever have to face the real issue. It is no different to over-eating, anorexia, alcoholism, gambling, or any other bad habit we develop in order to avoid feeling pain. Heavy stuff, isn't it? The mind is such a complex force, and has it's own unique way of letting us know that we have gone off course.

Once I accepted that my anxiety was present long before I ever made it to the post office and began listening to my heart, I had to reaffirm my own needs and recognise how I had been neglecting them. I once read about a man who suffered severe anxiety and had to quit his job. He began to attend counselling and was advised to take a half hour walk every day to relieve stress. After several months of looking after himself, talking to his counsellor and taking his walks, his stress levels reduced greatly. He was feeling so much better that he decided to return to work. Within two months he was back at the counsellors' office, as anxious as ever. The doctor asked him what he had been doing, and the man replied that he had returned to work but had to leave again because of the stress. The counsellor asked the man if he was still taking his walks, to which he replied that he was not, as he did not have the time. The counsellor asked him why he had stopped doing the very thing that was making him feel better, but of course the man had no response.

I also fell into that trap. I had worked for so long on doing all of the things that made me feel more comfortable in myself and less anxious. Yet, at the first sign of improvement, I dropped my new way of life like a hot potato in a rush to get back to my 'old self'. Of course it ended up in a setback and I was clueless as to how it had happened. They say some lessons are more difficult to learn than others and when I look at my most recent setback, I would have to say that I am still learning! However, once you become familiar with setbacks, you realise that they are only temporary and I can guarantee you that you feel a lot stronger when you come through it. Each setback is a lesson to be learned. I once heard an amusing comparison between the recovery process and a spiral staircase. You might keep coming round to the same spot, but you'll always be at a higher altitude!

So what about those days where you feel like the cartoon character with a grey cloud over your head? Sometimes a setback can set in for no apparent reason at all; sometimes there doesn't need to be a reason. Don't throw in the towel, all is not lost and it will not last forever. When I'm feeling less than average, I recognise that it is time to be extra kind and gentle with myself. Now is not the time to be facing fears or taking on the world, it is time to nurture yourself. You would not expect your car to run without any fuel and so it only stands to reason that you cannot expect your self to run without nourishment, or soul food, as I like to call it. There are as many different ways to nourish your soul, as there are stars in the sky. What makes you smile or brings a glow to your heart? What gives you a great sense of satisfaction or makes you feel good about yourself? I loved the quirkiness of the character Amélie in the movie 'Le Fabuleux Destin d'Amélie Poulain'. Her simple pleasures in life were dipping her fingers into sacks full of grain and skimming stones on the water. In our high tech world, so many of life's simple pleasures have lost their value, but why not take this opportunity to rediscover them? Here are some examples:

- Walk through the woods
- Go to the lake and feed the ducks
- Bake a cake just for yourself
- Go to the library and load up on books
- Watch a movie that always makes you laugh
- Read a glossy magazine
- Write a poem
- Have a picnic in the park
- Visit an art gallery
- Have a bath with extra bubbles
- Paint a sunset
- Change the colour of your bedroom walls
- Buy the really expensive ice-cream
- Do some gardening

You are probably wondering how the planting of a few shrubs can help with your feelings of anxiety and I have to admit that I did not see the connection myself either. However, it is not so much about what you are doing as the message you are sending yourself, which is that I MATTER! It is worth standing out on the edge of a pier throwing stale bread to the ducks because it makes me feel good about myself, and my happiness is a priority. Spending this kind of time doing activities that have no other purpose than to make us happy, increases our self worth and sense of priority. I baked a sponge cake the other day, just to see if I could do it. When I took it out from the oven and saw that it hadn't flopped, I had such a sense of satisfaction and achievement. Eating it was even better! Making these simple pleasures a part of your life has numerous benefits. You can learn a new hobby; learn about your own likes and dislikes, but most importantly, focus your energies on something other than anxiety.

So I hope that this chapter has shown the importance of experiencing setbacks. They are an alert signal to let us know that we have strayed off-track or lost sight of ourselves. This will happen, as we are not perfect and neither is the course of our recovery. We all want our graphs to have a straight line, but in reality, nothing in life is so clear-cut. It is a series of dips and curves with lessons to be learned and challenges to be met. It is worth remembering that life is like this for everyone, no one gets away without any scars. Suffering from an anxiety disorder can cause you to become quite self-absorbed, with the impression that no one faces the same difficulties and everyone else is content with their lot. This kind of thinking will only serve to make you feel even more isolated. Perhaps not everyone can identify with the exact kind of feelings produced by anxiety, but everyone knows what it is like to experience pain so you are not alone.

We are conned into believing that life is supposed to come wrapped up in neat little bows. On the contrary, life is messy and unfair. You had good days and bad days before anxiety and life will be no different now. You cannot eliminate all of the pain and suffering, but you can react to them differently and appreciate the good things all the more. Without getting too philosophical, I don't believe that we were put here merely to climb the corporate ladder, get a mortgage and pay our taxes. I think it is our purpose to learn, to experience and to reach our potential as thinking and feeling human beings. Without experiencing pain ourselves, how can we ever feel empathy for someone who is suffering? Without testing our limits, how will we know how far we can actually go? Without making mistakes, how will we ever learn? Well, that is my theory and I'm sticking to it!

8

The new you

Every cloud has a silver lining, and I believe that experiencing an anxiety disorder has many hidden blessings, if you're willing to search for them. Once I had pushed through the denial, the anger and finally acceptance, I found I was left with a magnificent blank canvas. All through my recovery, I had this recurring feeling that I had somehow lost my identity. I was right—I had, but it was not my identity to begin with. It was a version of me performing to other people's standards, wants and needs. Whether it was my parents, society, friends or employers, my identity seemed to gravitate towards what I thought was expected of me and how I thought I should act. The word 'should' no longer has a place in my vocabulary! Watch for it, it keeps creeping in there, trying to tell you what you *should* be doing rather than what you *want* to do. Avoid it at all costs!

So once I had unburdened myself of the shackles that bound me to my old way of life, which involved pleasing everybody but myself, I was free to paint a new picture and create the kind of life that made me happy. This is such a liberating experience, because, if you're anything like I was, constantly basing your decisions on other people's approval, the freedom to just do what you want is simply exhilarating! Thus begins the process of getting to know yourself, getting to know your likes and dislikes, saying no to those family reunions that you just hate and not feeling bad about it. Going to that pottery class and not feeling embarrassed when your high-flying friends ask you what you are doing with your time. Isn't it interesting how we place so little value on self-development and instead give great importance to career-development!

For the vast majority of us, it is very difficult to pinpoint exactly what we would like to do with our lives, basically because we've never really asked the question. I spent what seemed like a lifetime of falling into various office jobs, just because they were there and I needed the money, without any thought as to whether I actually liked that kind of work or not. This kind of thinking was an unfortunate consequence of my academic career, which focused solely on what kind of degree would get me a good job, rather than what I was actually interested in or drawn towards. I'm not being naive here, I realise we all need to make a living in order to survive, but imagine if it was possible to actually earn money while doing something you're remotely interested in? What a concept! A very useful book in helping you find your true calling in life is "What colour is your parachute" by Richard Bolles. It is very helpful if you are thinking of a career change or if you just want to find some new ideas for different career paths. I have to say my bible on this voyage of self-discovery has been "The Artist's Way" by Julia Cameron. I always knew I was drawn to the more creative side of life, but never had the courage to follow it through. This book is a twelve-week course designed to help you rediscover the creative soul within. It's actually the guiding light that continually spurred me ahead while writing this book. Whether you are creatively inclined or not, I think this book is beneficial to anyone going through a recovery process. It encourages self-belief and a lot of childlike indulgence!

As I mentioned at the beginning of this book, I can also see this process as a coming of age, a crossing into adulthood where we learn to choose our own destiny. It's time to take control back. Yes, we've been hurt, and our inner child is afraid and seeking protection. But what we need to realise is that we are the adults now, and we can take care of ourselves. I think this rite of passage should be marked with some basic rules, affirmations or just plain old human rights!

- I have the right to say NO
- I have the right to set boundaries
- I have the right to make my wants and needs a priority
- I have the right to be treated with respect
- I have the right to my own opinions
- I have the right to make mistakes
- I have the right to make my own decisions without the approval of others
- I have the right to refuse responsibility for other people
- I have the right to stand up for my beliefs and myself
- I have the right to express my feelings

One thing to remember is that our feelings of anxiety will never fully disappear. We would have a whole set of different problems if we did not have anxiety at all! It is a protective mechanism that only becomes harmful when it starts to get over-protective. As Susan Jeffers points out in her book *Feel The Fear And Do It Anyway*, 'The fear will never go away as long as I continue to grow.' I used to think that I would wake up one day and find that my anxiety had magically disappeared! It does not happen in this way. Rather, one day I woke up and decided that the pain of not doing something was worse than the anxiety experienced while doing it. I reasoned that even if I experienced anxiety while doing the thing I had feared, at least I could endorse myself for what I had done and would no longer feel like a helpless victim.

When I first began writing this book, I had hoped to finish it with a bang and regale you with stories of how I went on to master the universe! That was two years ago, and I have since realised that I don't want to take on the world; I just want to be myself. It takes a lot of courage to stand up for who you are and to follow the path less travelled, but when you are following your heart it is worth the effort. You will know when you are on the right path because there is a great sense of calm and contentment. At the beginning of this book, I referred to anxiety as our friend because it acts as an internal warning system, to let you know that you have gone off course.

I hope this book will become like an old friend that you can pick up and find comfort in, especially on the bad days. I have described this whole experience as the worst thing that ever happened to me and the best thing that ever happened to me. Yes, it was one of the biggest challenges of my life, but without it I would never have discovered my inner strength, courage and true identity. My new philosophy in life is very simple; I do my best and leave the rest up to God!

9
Inspirational writings

<u>A Blessing of Solitude</u>

May you recognise in your life the presence,
power and light of your soul.
May you realize that you are never alone that your soul in its brightness and
belonging connects you intimately with the rhythm of the universe.
May you have respect for your own individuality and difference.
May you realize that the shape of your soul is unique, that you have a special destiny here, that behind the facade of your life there is something beautiful, good
and eternal happening.
May you learn to see your self with the same delight, pride and expectation with
which God sees you in every moment.

John O'Donohue—*Anam Chara*
Spiritual Wisdom from the Celtic World

Our Deepest Fear

Is not that we are inadequate.
Our deepest fear is that we are powerful beyond measure.
It is our light, not our darkness, that most frightens us.
We ask ourselves, who am I to be brilliant, gorgeous, talented and fabulous?
Actually, who are you not to be?
You are a child of God.
Your playing small doesn't serve the world.
There's nothing enlightened about shrinking so that other people won't feel insecure around you.
We were born to make manifest the glory of God that is within us.
It's not just in some of us:
It's in Everyone!
And as we let our own light shine, we unconsciously give other people permission to do the same.
As we are liberated from our own fear, our presence automatically liberates others.

From Nelson Mandela's inaugural speech—1994

References

Mental Health Through Will Training—Willett Publishing Illinois 1986
Dr. Abraham Low

How To Control Your Anxiety Before It Controls You—Carol Publishing N.J. 1998
Albert Ellis PhD

Triumph Over Fear—Bantam 1995
Jerilyn Ross

Stress Control—Pan Books London 1978
Vernon Coleman

Six Pillars of Self Esteem—Bantam 1995
Nathaniel Branden

The Hidden Face of Shyness : Understanding & Overcoming Social Anxiety—Harper Collins 1996
Franklin Schneier MD, Lawrence Welkowitz PhD

Beyond Codependency : And Getting Better All The Time—Health Communications Inc.
Melody Beattie

The Artist's Way—Pan Books U.K. 1995
Julia Cameron

Feel The Fear And Do It Anyway—Random House UK 1987
Susan Jeffers

Home Coming—Piatkus U.K. 1999
John Bradshaw

The Self You Have To Live With—Unwin, London 1938
Winfred Rhoades

Anam Chara—Bantam Press U.K. 1997
John O'Donohue

978-0-595-36436-7
0-595-36436-5

CAUSES

BODY SENDING A MESSAGE

DUE TO UNRESOLVED FEELINGS

RESPONSES

BE YOURSELF

ACCEPT YOUR FAULTS

SHARE YOUR FEELINGS